WISP

By Cynthia Rider

Illustrated by Dick Bogie

CAMBRIDGE
UNIVERSITY PRESS

It's time for the Dog Show
at Aspen Town Hall.
There are dogs who are big
and dogs who are small.

2

There are dogs who are plump
with tails that go thump,
and dogs who are grumpy
and down-in-the-dumps.

3

There are dogs who are good,
and dogs who are scamps,
and all of them want to be
this year's Show Champ.

4

But just as the Show
is about to begin,
there's a bump and a thump
and a big dog jumps in.

5

It's Big Bob the Bully.
He stands in the hall,
and he says, "I'm the Champ.
I'm the best dog of all!"

6

"Go away," says the judge.
"Big Bob, you must go.
You cannot come in.
You will spoil the Dog Show."

7

Big Bob stamps his feet.
He says, "No, I won't go.
I want to be Champ
of this year's Dog Show."

8

Then into the hall
comes Annabel Crisp,
and after her trots
her little dog, Wisp.

Big Bob looks at Wisp,
and he yelps,
"What is that! Is it a rat,
or a mat, or a hat?

10

Is it a spider,
or is it a mop?
Or is it a wig
with a bow on the top?"

11

Wisp runs at Big Bob.
She gives him a thump.
She yaps and she snaps.
She makes Big Bob jump.

She nips his black nose.
She stamps on his toes.
Big Bob starts to yelp,
"Get her off me! Help! Help!"

Wisp chases Big Bob
away from the hall.
He yelps and he gulps.
He jumps over the wall.

Then Annabel Crisp
picks her little dog up.
The judge says, "Well done, Wisp!
You have won this big cup!"

15

Then the dogs yelp and yap
and the people all cheer.
Wisp is the Champ.
She's Top Dog of the Year!